# MICROCOSM·PUBLISHING

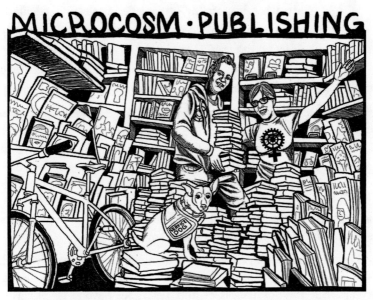

**Microcosm Publishing** is Portland's most diversified publishing house and distributor, with a focus on the colorful, authentic, and empowering. Our books and zines have put your power in your hands since 1996, equipping readers to make positive changes in their lives and in the world around them. Microcosm emphasizes skill-building, showing hidden histories, and fostering creativity through challenging conventional publishing wisdom with books and bookettes about DIY skills, food, bicycling, gender, self-care, and social justice. What was once a distro and record label started by Joe Biel in a drafty bedroom was determined to be *Publishers Weekly*'s fastest-growing publisher of 2022 and #3 in 2023, and is now among the oldest independent publishing houses in Portland, OR, and Cleveland, OH. We are a politically moderate, centrist publisher in a world that has inched to the right for the past 80 years.

# INTRODUCTION

*T*he mysteries of sleep have eluded us for many centuries, with the early Egyptians and other cultures giving us clues into what lies on the other side of sleep, particularly in relation to death, dreams, and awakenings. Many people sleep without a second thought; they simply go to bed one day and wake up fresh and rejuvenated on another. But for some of us, those hours between one day and the next are plagued by an array of nocturnal phenomena and so-called sleep disorders.

Sleep paralysis has shaped the person that I am today. I had no prior experience with any type of spiritual or religious practice, but my personal struggle with sleep paralysis has taken me on a journey of self-exploration that has led me to pursue a PhD, with a focus on researching the sociological impact of this phenomenon. Sleep paralysis has, in essence, become the focal point of my life, whether I'm experiencing it first-hand or examining it as a researcher.

This zine shines a light on the phenomenon of sleep paralysis, which has existed without exploration of its spiritual context for thousands of years. But the uniqueness of this text goes beyond sleep paralysis. It explores the very nature of human "beingness," as it opens the door to a real discussion about the dimensional nature of us as humans, the potential of other realities and the nonphysical energies within the Universe.

This zine thereby creates a bridge between what is called a sleep disorder, spirituality, metaphysics, and the paranormal, and it explains how some of us are uniquely born to experience all four. It will bring you to a place of knowing that you are far more than what you think you are, and that far more exists beyond the veil of sleep.

It is important to recognize at this stage, that due to the complex interweaving of neurology, physiology, consciousness, and spirituality with your unique makeup, the sleep paralysis experience, whilst having consistent features, constitutes a blend of your thought patterns, expectations, and experiences. During sleep paralysis, you will experience what you expect, which in most cases is fear based—hence the approach taken in this zine of focussing on your health and wellbeing. It is by taking this approach that you are able to control your expectations and the experiences during sleep paralysis and ultimately realize the gift.

This is not a book of spells or mystical rituals to help rid yourself of sleep paralysis. It has instead been designed to not only help you transcend sleep paralysis but to also help you understand your physical and nonphysical self in intimate detail, ensuring that you work towards attaining your highest spiritual alignment, and that by doing so you gain access to the spiritual gifts that are waiting for you. For those who seek knowledge relating to their general spiritual development, this text provides an ideal introduction to your spiritual growth, giving you insights into what is possible.

This zine is organized into three parts. Part One covers the fundamentals of sleep paralysis and explores how it's been commonly understood and treated. Part Two reframes sleep paralysis as a spiritual phenomenon and explains how shifting your energetic frequency can liberate you from your struggle against it. Positive affirmations are also included throughout Part Two, to support you in raising your frequency to transcend sleep paralysis. Finally, Part Three is more action-oriented: it lays out 18 actionable steps that you can take to support your spiritual development and overcome your difficulties with sleep paralysis.

This will be a journey of discovery, transformation, and empowerment. Let's begin.

# PART ONE: THE FOUNDATIONS

## Chapter 1. The Fundamentals of Sleep Paralysis

For those who experience sleep paralysis, the phenomenon causes anxiety and thoughts about the existence of other-worldly, spiritual, and ghoulish entities that show themselves during sleep. Whispering the words "sleep paralysis" provokes either curiosity and a desire to know more about it, or an uncomfortable feeling, a shift in emotional balance that leads to tensions as the listener recalls things they have heard or read about the phenomenon. Without a doubt, sleep paralysis has received bad press over the past few thousand years, and now is the time to remove the negative connotations that prevent a broader understanding of the topic. Together we will be delving deep to explore sleep paralysis and its spiritual connections. We will be unmasking the mystery, exposing that which is hidden beneath the cloud of terror experienced during the phenomenon.

Let's begin by determining what we do and don't know about sleep paralysis. Up to 62 percent of the global population has had at least one episode of sleep paralysis.[1] According to Dr. David Hufford,[2] researcher of extraordinary spiritual experiences, the phenomenon is characterized by some or all of the following experiences during sleep:

- The sleeper senses and/or sees an evil presence in the room, which is threatening and intimidating

- The sleeper feels that they are being touched, choked, or strangled

- The sleeper feels something pressing down on their chest or abdomen

- Panic, fear, and terror are experienced

- The sleeper is unable to move a muscle or utter a sound, creating the feeling of paralysis

- The sleeper awakens with clear recognition of the experience and an awareness of it being a "real" event

1 M Dahlitz and JD Parkes, "Sleep Paralysis," *Lancet*, 341 (February 1993): 406-407.
2 David J. Hufford, "Sleep Paralysis as Spiritual Experience," *Transcultural Psychiatry* 42, no. 1 (March 2005).

To anyone who has not experienced sleep paralysis, this definition of something taking place as a real physical experience sounds totally ridiculous, impossible, and even incomprehensible. The normal response is "they must have been dreaming" or "they're going through a stressful time which triggered a nightmare or hallucination." The more spiritually attuned person may just go silent when hearing the explanation, unsure of how to respond.

Medical and sleep experts do not know why sleep paralysis occurs and suggest that it happens during REM (Rapid Eye Movement) sleep. This is when the body's muscles are immobile and unresponsive. In this sleep state, all muscles are unable to move. It's a safety mechanism to ensure that we don't act out our dreams and harm ourselves. The sleep paralysis experience is said to happen at the end of REM sleep before waking, or when entering it. While this may be true in some instances, from experience, I can clearly state that this is not always the case, as some episodes have taken place before I entered REM sleep, even seconds after I have gone to sleep.

But, how is it explained when these "nightmares" happen over and over again, night after night? When there are no "stressful situations" or personal problems? When the individual is perfectly healthy and balanced and everything in their life is going well? Surely, there has to be more to this phenomenon.

We do know that sleep paralysis has been experienced for many hundreds of years, with its first formal written recognition found in the American Academy of Sleep Medicine's first publication in 1979,3 where it was classified as a "sleep and arousal" disorder. Going back even further, there are accounts of sleep paralysis in Persia in 983 AD,4 and in 1781 Henry Fuseli highlighted sleep paralysis in an oil painting. In this painting he depicts a demonic incubus sitting on a sleeping woman's chest, her arms and head thrown above her, whilst a black horse looks on. The implication is subtly sexual, and the scene feels familiar to the sleep paralysis experiencer.

Fuseli called the painting *The Nightmare*, and when we look at the definition of the word, it was said in the late 13th century to be "an evil female spirit afflicting sleepers with a feeling of suffocation," a compound of the words "night" and "mare." The word "mare" was derived from Anglo Saxon folklore where the "mare" or "old horse" rides on sleepers'

---

3 "Diagnostic Classification of Sleep and Arousal Disorders," *Sleep* 2, no. 1 (1979).
4 Samad Ej Golzari et al. "Sleep paralysis in Medieval Persia: The Hidayat of Akhawayni (?-983 AD)," *Neuropsychiatric Disease and Treatment* 8 (2012): 229-34.

chests and suffocates them. Nightmares, we find, are derived from the sleep paralysis experience, quite literally.

Today, those who experience sleep paralysis normally keep their experiences to themselves. They are apprehensive about discussing it, for several reasons: fear of being misunderstood, of being an outcast, fear of appearing evil, strange or weird, and even fear of being likened to having an infectious disease that must be kept secret so they can continue to be "normal." Privately they search for help, with Google search after Google search, bookstore after bookstore, hoping to find what isn't there. The sufferer will avoid doctors with their "spooky" illness (unless it becomes absolutely unbearable), and doctors, who are determined to avoid spiritual mysticism, are focused on conventional methods. Many do not know what to do about it, and many have never heard of it before—as a medical condition, that is.

Cultures all over the world have folklore, fables, and tales representing sleep paralysis. In Germany, there are tales of hags or horses, who are demons and witches, possessing people while they sleep. Stories from Newfoundland speak of the Old Hag that comes at night and sits on sleepers' chests. Japan has the kanashibari, which causes terror and paralysis. The experiences are worldwide, with no apparent exclusion criteria.

The life of someone who experiences sleep paralysis is plagued with constant fatigue due not only to lack of sleep, but also to disturbed sleep, as the sleep paralysis events can take place several times during the night, waking up the sleeper each time. It's also important to note that as there is no determinant of regularity, they can take place weekly, bi-monthly, or yearly. Or for some, once in a blue moon. In my case, I could guarantee that I would have an episode every 2-3 days. "They're going to get me whilst I sleep," was my silent call that no one understood but me. For the uninitiated: if you have a sleep paralysis episode once, they have the potential to take place again.

Fear of sleeping, fear of the dark, and fear of the nighttime are common emotions, with the affected person often staying awake as long as possible, hoping that the later it gets the less the chances of having an episode will be. Sleeping with the light on is another common reaction as the shame and despair of the secret situation continues. We know that the experience is frightening and that while we sleep we have almost no control over what takes place. This is an experience shared by many: all across the world, reports of the phenomenon are strikingly similar—the similarities are undeniable. And it's important to note that your physical and psychological experiences with sleep paralysis are symptoms of the phenomenon and not the cause. In the chapters that follow, we will explore possible causes of sleep paralysis and discover why physiological and psychological explanations are insufficient.

# Chapter 2. Explanations and Solutions

Sleep experts and the medical community, including the National Health Service in the United Kingdom and the Sleep Foundation, have proposed several possible causes of sleep paralysis. These fall into three main areas: sleep deprivation, psychological stress, and abnormal sleep cycles. Each of these areas has been thoroughly researched. Let's explore them in more detail.

## SLEEP DEPRIVATION

When the body does not receive the required amount of sleep and experiences a range of symptoms, it is said to be sleep-deprived. The average amount of sleep that is necessary each night for peak physical and mental performance is six to eight hours. Receiving less than this for a sustained period of time can lead to chronic illnesses such as high blood pressure, heart disease, and weight gain. Sleep deprivation can also affect the brain and cognitive functions.

Symptoms of sleep deprivation include fatigue, sleepiness during the daytime, irritability, and, in some circumstances, irrational behavior. It is notable that sleep deprivation can be a symptom of sleep paralysis as well as the cause, and while the symptoms of sleep deprivation can also be caused by sleep paralysis, this does not explain why the sleep paralysis would occur as a result of sleep deprivation or why everyone who experiences sleep deprivation does not experience sleep paralysis. The entities which we all see during these episodes and the pressure on the chest, which seems to be a significant part of the experience, are also not addressed by this explanation.

## PSYCHOLOGICAL STRESS

Severe stress can trigger episodes of sleep paralysis. While experts are not sure of the connection between the two, everyday stresses such as those related to work, health, or relationships are said by sleep and medical experts to be causal factors. Very little is known about the connection between sleep paralysis and stress, but this indicator has been present in a portion of cases, and again, not everyone who experiences stress experiences sleep paralysis, and vice versa.

## Abnormal Sleep Cycles

Having an internal clock that is out of alignment does not allow for "normal" sleep patterns. This is classified by the medical community as having an abnormal sleep cycle. When there is no clear sleep cycle and sleep is broken into pieces, the person may feel sleepy, take naps during the day, and be wide awake at night. This is a rare condition. The internal clock needs to be reset, as this prolonged sleep habit can become the norm and the body becomes accustomed to sleeping in this way. Unfortunately, this is also a result of sleep paralysis, as a sleep paralysis episode can be experienced at any time of the day or night and disrupt sleep patterns.

## Other Possible Causes

Outside of the three main areas above, additional factors that can contribute to sleep paralysis include sleeping on your back, and overuse of stimulants and certain medications such as those used to treat ADHD. There is also a strong connection between Narcolepsy (a neurological disorder that impedes the brain's ability to manage sleep cycles) and sleep paralysis.

There is a clear need for more research into sleep paralysis. For the moment, these suggestions have been tested and researched and have, for some, provided a degree of relief:

- Not sleeping on your back: Sleeping on your back seems to stimulate the attacks. The reason for this is not clear, but avoiding sleeping on your back seems to reduce the frequency of episodes.

- Good sleep hygiene. Good sleep practices and routines are said to improve the quality of sleep and reduce the frequency of sleep paralysis episodes. These practices include going to sleep and waking up at the same time each day, keeping active and exercising regularly, staying away from particular types of food and drink that are known to disturb sleep, (for example, caffeine), and ensuring that your bed and sheets are comfortable and that the room is suitably dark.

- Reducing or avoiding the use of tobacco and alcohol. While this is fairly obvious, tobacco and alcohol are substances that can disturb sleep. For anyone who experiences sleep paralysis, these are toxins which give the sleeper a deeper sleep than would normally be experienced.

- Relaxing and applying muscle relaxation techniques. This includes diaphragmatic breathing, mindfulness, progressive muscle relaxation, and meditation. All of these are to enable better coping strategies during an attack. The theory is that the more relaxed the individual is, the easier it is to slip out of REM sleep and wake up.

- During an experience, attempt a small movement of an extremity, like a finger or toe. A small movement can break the "spell" and allow you to wake up easily.

Some health professionals have tried to treat sleep paralysis in a roundabout way by helping the patient with their anxiety and sleep hygiene. In extreme cases, cognitive behavioral therapy is used. This was one of the first published and earliest treatments for sleep paralysis, and it is also sometimes used to treat insomnia. This technique involves identifying thoughts or behaviors that can worsen your sleep.

While these approaches are said to help, they do not entirely cure sleep paralysis. Treatment options for sleep paralysis are poorly studied, with very little understanding. Research into sleep paralysis is poorly funded, with the academic community shying away from the notion that it might be a spiritual or metaphysical occurrence. This leaves almost no treatment options. Many experiencers end up in a vicious cycle: they avoid sleep and therefore inadvertently bring on a sleep disorder that is said to cause sleep paralysis.

For some who experience sleep paralysis, the search for a cure does not stop and extreme and unconventional methods are tested. I tried so many, including sleeping with the light on, keeping Bibles all over the house, burning incense and oils, sleeping in different beds in the house, moving the furniture around, moving into a different house, prayer, attending church, being blessed by pastors, and staying awake during the night. Looking back at these, they seem a little extreme now, but they were fueled by my belief that evil spiritual entities were lying in wait for me to sleep so that they could attack me. My belief in the devil and the forces of good and evil led me to try all sorts of remedies in the hope that I could "cast away" the evil spirits. But I came to know that it had nothing to do with my bedroom, the house, my sleep hygiene, nor my religious inclinations. It was all about me. I was at the center of it all and, ultimately, I could not escape from myself. I had to live with it. When all other options were exhausted, I stopped trying to solve the problem. In making the decision to live with it, I found the solution.

It is common, however, to try to mask sleep paralysis with drugs and therapy without understanding what it is and why it occurs. But while the symptoms are uncomfortable to say the least, there must be a reason why they occur and why not everyone experiences sleep paralysis. What actually takes place during an episode? Is it a nonphysical spiritual engagement or is it a hallucination as medical research suggests? As a seasoned sleep paralysis experiencer, I would have to agree with the former. And when I made the decision to stop fighting against my sleep paralysis, I also had to recognize that my perception of evil needed to be reframed, as I was now entering the realm of spirituality. I asked myself, Am I perceiving this spiritual visitation as evil simply because of the intellectual framework of "evil" that I have built? How can I shift past this perception? And what does the spiritual entity want? I needed to know what it was all about, to understand it and myself in the process. It was a covert exercise in understanding my inner self. I began a search to know and understand more.

# PART TWO: CHANGING YOUR RELATIONSHIP WITH SLEEP PARALYSIS

## Chapter 3. Embracing the Gifts

*I*n the preceding chapters, you learned what sleep paralysis is and explored the commonly understood causes and remedies. By now you understand that sleep experts and the medical community actually know very little about this global phenomenon. Sustained treatments for sleep paralysis are nonexistent, despite the millions of people each year who experience repeat episodes. Approaching sleep paralysis from a practical, action-orientated, physical-world approach has yielded very few results.

With that understanding, it's time for us to seriously explore the spiritual or supernatural nature of sleep paralysis. We can cast aside the documented explanations for sleep paralysis and consider the following possibility:

*Sleep paralysis is a symptom of a spiritual awakening. When episodes take place, the sleeper is being visited to be given a gift that they have not yet accepted.*

This is a bold statement. It embraces sleep paralysis rather than attempting to alleviate or cure it. It presents the idea that the sleeper is a benefactor of sleep paralysis. This allows us to approach the episodes from a position of worthiness wherein we accept the gifts that are being offered, rather than a position of fear wherein we reject what is happening. The nonphysical gifts transcend and by far outweigh anything that can be given in the physical world. These include the gifts of enlightenment and empowerment. They also include psychic abilities, such as heightened intuition and knowing (often referred to as claircognizance), extreme sensitivity to emotions (empathy), and an awareness of future events or the ability to see situations with extreme clarity (clairvoyance). With these gifts comes an elevated sense of having abilities that are not granted to everyone and of being in touch with something extraordinary. A superpower has surfaced, and if we are asked to be without the gifts we answer with a resounding "no," because returning to being a "normal" individual seems shallow and diminished. We are immediately released from the need to stop the episodes; instead, we are tasked with accepting that there is something of value about us, which causes us to have these experiences. The sleep deprivation and frustrations experienced previously begin to subside together with the fear and avoidance of sleep. The empowered state brings with it a willingness to experience sleep paralysis so that the journey into the unknown can continue.

When confronted with this possibility, most people feel a sense of relief. This is because most of us who experience sleep paralysis know that something that cannot be defined, categorized, or rationalized is taking place. We know that our intuition is crying out for us to pay attention, but in this real world of tangibles and physical action, it's easier to ignore our intuition—that is, until the symptoms of ignoring it become unbearable, manifesting as sleep paralysis.

Once we view the experience through this lens, there is no longer a need for us to try to convince ourselves that it was a hallucination. We don't need to incessantly pray or undertake protective rituals before retiring to bed. We are now free to take back our personal power, focus on ourselves, and begin the process of self-transformation to release the fear and resistance that prevents us from accepting the gift we are offered.

Shifting to this viewpoint is therefore a pivotal moment in our spiritual journey. In this chapter, we will begin to delve more deeply into what that shift looks like.

## MAKING THE SHIFT

Anyone who experiences sleep paralysis has a predisposition toward receiving spiritual energy that vibrates at a high level. This is the energy of spiritual awakenings and advancement. It's the energy of empowerment and knowing who you are. Sleep paralysis defines you as someone who has the capacity to receive the gift, and with some toning of that spiritual muscle, the gift can be delivered. You have been chosen to receive the gift and the nightly visits are your wake-up call. For this wake-up call to be effective, you must be willing to at least explore your spirituality. This is not a verbal or physical act. It is a deeply personal and emotional act. Your spirituality is extremely sensitive to your emotions, so the intention is to be emotionally ready.

Next, you need to make a decision to face the demons or whatever is presented in your sleep state. After all, what choice do you have? You can either continue to run from it or face it head on. This starts with recognizing that you have a choice and the power to transform your experience with sleep paralysis—instead of listening to the voice that tells you this is something to be feared. In this spiritual world, fear attracts more fear, and a life filled with perpetual fear, sleeplessness, anxiety, and stress will continue until you decide to break the cycle.

Sleep paralysis does not happen randomly; it is specific and purposeful. Once you embrace the gift, sleeping without sleep paralysis episodes will be the least of the benefits. The gift and your alignment have immense potential for your health, wellbeing, and life in general. You will find that you have more vitality and energy. Your outlook towards your life will shift dramatically as you embrace all possibilities and see yourself as invincible. An inner unshakeable peace and ability to deal with all that life brings you will arrive, along with trust and knowing that nothing is meaningless and that everything is for your wellbeing. Your clarity and focus will increase as you begin to feel inspired from within, rather than seek external motivation and validation. Your psychic abilities will pale in comparison to your happiness, joy, and focus on all that is important. You now view all life holistically because you can see your role in the universe and all that it has to offer. While you will be part of the everyday mundane world, you will understand that the Universe and all its secrets is within you and that you have the ability to experience and know things that others do not. And therein lies the gift.

## CONFIDENCE AND SELF-LOVE

People who don't experience sleep paralysis will often trivialize the episodes without realizing it. It's difficult for them to relate to the experience. In an attempt to help, they offer rational explanations for the episodes together with remedies: "You're overworked or stressed. Get a good night's sleep and you'll be fine." While the intentions are compassionate, friends and family really can't help when it comes to sleep paralysis.

As you begin to accept your predicament and develop your spiritual strength, you will be willing to let others judge and critique you. You will have self-love. With this love comes a feeling of invincibility. No one thing is too great for you. This translates into your everyday life as you begin to notice changes in your thinking and in your behavior. You no longer care about what others think or say about you. People around you can judge you, talk about you, accuse you, or point fingers at you. All this means nothing to you, as you are absorbed and focused on yourself. No longer are you a "yes person," trying to please and keep up with others. You become confident and self-assured. Those around you begin to notice changes in your behavior as you become sure, focused, and selfish—not the type of selfish that acts to the detriment of anyone, but the type that acts to your own benefit as you treat yourself like a precious jewel.

## FACING THE CONSTRUCT OF EVIL

Historically, sleep paralysis has been portrayed and experienced as an evil phenomenon. I can clearly understand why, as the episode itself often makes it seem that an evil entity is attempting to do you harm. As explained in earlier chapters, folklore confirms this: hundreds of tales from across the world all state the same thing. The media portrays sleep paralysis as devilish, with social media leading the way in graphic detail. To shift from viewing this energy as evil to viewing it as pure love is a difficult concept to grasp, especially when sleep paralysis causes such terror.

So what will it take for you to have this positive experience? First, it requires a shift in thinking.

We have all unconsciously adopted social constructs and have a shared perception of the devil, demons, and evil entities which have been created and shared by societies throughout the world. We then change our thoughts and feelings towards these constructs as the process of self-transformation gets underway. As members of society, we have bought into assumed truths which need to be dismantled and rebuilt if we are to reach a higher level of understanding and overcome the struggle against sleep paralysis.

You'll address the assumption that sleep paralysis is evil as your understanding and awareness of the events widens to encompass alternative views. There is no need to concern yourself with the thought that the entities will attack you more if you do not oppose them. These thoughts are based on fear, and it is this fear which you need to overcome and supersede with thoughts of accomplishment and worthiness. You are on a journey of self-empowerment which has no room for fear-based thoughts. Self-love is the core of facing your fears, as at all times you must demand the best for yourself, and facing the fear and removing fear-based thoughts are part of the process of empowerment and enlightenment.

## CONCLUSION

This chapter has planted a seed: The idea that sleep paralysis could be a gift that is being presented, but not yet accepted. To accept the gift, there is some work to be done. This work essentially focuses on enhancing your spirituality and preparing yourself emotionally. With your spiritual development comes not only the gift, but also your self-love, worthiness, and happiness. By developing your spirituality and self-love you expand your contribution to society, and the universe.

Accepting the spiritual nature of your being is central to relieving sleep paralysis, and the significance of this step cannot be overstated. This process is extremely positive and opens you up to endless possibilities, but it is a personal matter and one that you may ponder for several months. Starting to see yourself as special and unique, with a gift being offered to you, may be a completely new concept which you are beginning to explore. Your worthiness and internal power is being called to the forefront as sleep paralysis is requesting that you strengthen these muscles and begin the process of self-love and putting your own needs first. You now need to get into the driver's seat.

Part of your transformation encompasses understanding spiritual energy—not only your own energy, but that of others around you. The next chapter explains this energy and how it is integrated into your very being and that of everything else around you.

### Affirmations to Practice:

- I will sleep peacefully and awaken refreshed and rejuvenated

- I will reduce my resistance and allow myself to receive the gifts each episode offers me

# Chapter 4. Energy and Sleep

*T*here is so much going on in our waking and sleeping experience that we are unaware of, and yet it exists alongside us, forever present and unacknowledged. There are so many things that share our physical space that our senses do not perceive. Yet during brief moments, for those of us who are fortunate, the worlds exist in the same space, and the other side is witnessed and experienced. The sleep state gives us the ability to peek behind our normal "vision" and lift the veil that divides worlds. Our physical senses during our wake state are not "tuned or sensitive" enough to pick up or receive the existence of this other "world," therefore, the vast majority of us are oblivious to its existence. No map exists with a secret code for finding this other world. There are no hidden paths or gateways. The only way to experience what is unseen is to become attuned to it, which the sleep paralysis experiencer has already unintentionally done, to some extent. This attunement is the crux of this chapter.

We really know very little of what takes place when we sleep, and we take our vulnerability or opportunity for granted. However, there is opportunity in the unknown. Those of us who experience sleep paralysis have been given entry into the abyss of the nonphysical sleep realm. Just as the Universe is an endless expanse, so too is the sleep realm. And as sleep paralysis teaches us, there are many mysteries to understand and translate into everyday language.

## MAKING SENSE OF THE SLEEP STATE

Our waking experience is filled with activity from the moment we awake. We make sense of the world through that which we can see, touch, hear, feel, and smell and these things have been given titles and associated feelings that fit into the constructs discussed in the previous chapter. This process helps us to make sense of the world and where we fit in it. With these constructs we have shared understanding, perceptions, and emotions that allow us to relate with each other as a global society.

These constructs are also taken into the sleep realm and allow us to make sense of the sleep world. We really have no other tool with which to understand what takes place while we sleep, and we are often confused by the sleep realm, due to its inconsistencies with the constructs and patterns of behavior that we understand. The sleep realm operates under a different set of rules. In the sleep state we can do things which are impossible to do when we are awake, we have abilities and skills that are yet to be conceived in the waking state. This is why we recall very little of what takes place while we sleep, as our dogmatic minds can not adjust to the differing principles.

We attempt to make the dream realm fit into our understanding of the waking realm, without realizing that this is like hot and cold, chalk and cheese. The sleep state is a nonphysical dimension. We go to sleep in one realm and resurface in another. In this other realm the laws of physics as we know them, do not exist. Here, energies which are ever present in our waking world can easily interact and communicate with us because we are without resistance in this realm. The stressors and activities which dominated your thoughts while you were awake, have been put on pause. When you do wake, you search for remnants of the previous day, then pick them up and continue where you left off.

In the sleeping world, your physical body is vulnerable, and so too is your spiritual self, which is dominant not only when you sleep, but all the time. It's just that for the vast majority of people, this spiritual self is subdued and ignored as we go through our day. Our minds are full of thoughts that block out the divine communication that is constantly trying to be heard, through unacknowledged senses such as our intuition or the whispers in our mind.

Fortunately, it is during our sleep that this communication can take place undisturbed, albeit not always understood.

## FREQUENCY AND VIBRATION
Everything in existence has a frequency. The rate at which an object vibrates can change to be either higher or lower. A higher or faster vibration equates to positivity, while a slower vibration equates to lower energy and negativity. Greater spiritual enlightenment is aligned with higher vibrations.

Energy that is constantly around us also vibrates at a unique frequency. When we are in a group setting, there is a multitude of energies emanating from the people around us. Added to this, energy does not dissipate, it merely changes, but can never be extinguished. The energy that is within us as human beings does not suddenly disappear when we pass away, it remains, albeit in a different form. During the sleep state this energy has an opportunity to interact with us in our energetic form, and us with it.

The sleep paralysis experience can also include the "out of body" (sometimes referred to as astral projection) and "lucid dreaming" (where you know that you're dreaming while you're sleeping) states. Each of these is the result of energetic manipulation while you are in an energetic or nonphysical state. The sleep state is an ideal environment for energetic interaction. **It's us physical beings, with our limited awareness and conceptual understanding of the spiritual energetic world, that complicate the interaction by panicking and characterizing the experience as evil.**

## YOUR SPIRITUAL ENERGY

The nature of us as human spiritual beings has been well documented. Many spiritual speakers from differing approaches say the same thing: that we are spiritual in the first instance, with the human physical body providing a carapace for the magnificent spiritual energy that is the real you.

This spiritual energy varies from person to person, to the extent that no two people's energies are alike. The energy gauge measures from low to high with no minimum or maximum. The determinants of your energy level are many and vary from moment to moment. They include the following:

a) General mood

b) Responses and actions throughout the day

c) Clarity, awareness, thoughtfulness, and mindfulness

Each of the above is to some extent superficial, because although spiritual energy has the ability to fluctuate in either direction, it also stabilizes to its preferred level for each person, like water in a bottle that is shaken—it is easy for it to level back out to its original state. Having said that, once the energy has risen, it is fairly easy to keep it at a heightened level with changes in mindset and practical tools.

When it comes to spiritual energy, you also need to factor in the energies which are ever present and interacting with each of us constantly. Everything consists of energy and includes those of people and animals around you. Your physical environment also has these interacting energies which move, fluctuate, and mix with us unceasingly, impacting our spiritual energy constantly.

Spiritual energy levels increase incrementally, providing you with more connections to the spiritual realm, which by default also provides access to infinite intelligence. For some, this would translate to your guardian angels or spiritual guides, but whatever you want to call them, they are ever present and constantly calling to you through your intuition, signs, increased perception, or synchronicities. Fortunately, there are specific actions that you can take to increase your awareness of the calling. The more you focus on clarity, awareness, thoughtfulness, and mindfulness the higher your energy level will be in that moment. Your attention will be in the present moment, not the past or the future, thereby reducing your resistance and possible anxieties and allowing the energies to flow without blockage. Meditation is an excellent practice for maintaining awareness of the present moment, which is why it is widely used, not only for general health benefits but also to increase your spiritual energy and connection with the broader energy or source.

The broader external energies (we will call this source spiritual energy for now) vibrate at an extremely high frequency, much higher than our own, which is why it is often difficult for us to clearly interact with this energy and hear the guidance that is being offered. But the wonderful thing about this process is that the source spiritual energy never becomes impatient. It never tires or decides not to guide you, even though most of the time you are not listening. It never complains or becomes fed up with your behavior, nor does it criticize you, put you down, or condemn you.

The essence of this source energy is pure love. Words on this paper cannot express the depth of this love. It is encompassing, wholesome, and ever present and most of all it is non-compromising, non-negotiable, and consistent. Source energy loves you above all things, you are the focus of its attention and it wants the best for you at all times regardless of what you do. When you criticize yourself it is silently saying the opposite, when you doubt yourself it is silently encouraging you, and when you are depressed it is forever calling you to reach for more.

## Connections Between Sleep and the Spirit World

It is during the sleep state that you experience this source energy in a different form, as it swoons and swerves in the united pool of everyone's source energy. And by everyone's source energy, I'm referring to the energy of persons who are still alive and those who have passed on. Energy does not dissipate. It is forever constant.

This pool therefore consists of all energy. In this pool all energy overlaps, mixes, and merges, so that we are all one. Yet the irony is that while we are all one, we are all also individuals with our own unique energy signature.

While you sleep, the energetic part of you gets to glimpse the spiritual world. For some of us the experience is seamless, and we awaken none the wiser, with only whispers of the events that took place, but there are some of us who have a far more intense experience as the source spiritual energy attempts to engage us at a higher energetic level. During this experience the external source spiritual energy is calling you. The pool has combined with your spiritual energy and a team has united to call you. But are you ready?

As mentioned previously, during our wake state we are constantly bombarded with information and busy with action. We are not listening, not hearing the call. The energies that surround us during the day have limited access to an individual's consciousness due to resistance, distractions, and constricted thoughts, and find that during the sleep state we are more relaxed and receptive to the integration with this higher-level frequency. When we sleep, tensions decrease, we relax and release our hold on things which were important during the waking realm. Our spiritual source and the united energy are now dominant. We are in their world playing catch-up to understand all that takes place.

While you sleep, due to your heightened and focused frequency, the broader source energies try to engage you—to capture your attention as they would in the daytime—but the energy level you are emitting at that time is too low for you to comprehend the experience. You enter into a state of shock, which is compounded by the body's physiological response of paralysis, and you awaken in the spiritual or dream realm, unable to comprehend what has taken place. The shock of the experience throws you into a state of fear and panic, which can be likened to being thrown into a cold bath.

While in shock, the mind creates a framework for the fear that is based upon concepts that took years to build. Suffocation and paralysis is experienced, and entities are seen as the mind tries to make sense of the experience. The experience is real, albeit in another dimension, as you see the gatekeepers who are determined to prevent you from venturing further. The mind tries to protect itself from the experience, by falling back on social constructs as the energy tries to interact and gain your attention—but fear hijacks the experience. You unwittingly reject the energy, interpreting it negatively, as you force yourself awake saying: "What the hell just happened?"

What is to be emphasized here is that there is something special about you which gives you the capacity to tune into your source energy (and that of other people and the wider source energy), albeit unconsciously and unobtrusively. Your subtle empathic, intuitive, clairvoyant, or claircognizant abilities are the tell-tale signs of deeper spiritual abilities that led to your predisposition to engage with the spiritual realm and experience sleep paralysis. Only those with the spiritual acuity to attune to the vibrational frequency to engage "sleep paralysis" will have the experience. Once you become aware of this, your perception of the experience will change from negative to positive, and you will see yourself as part of an exclusive minority.

## CONCLUSION

At the center of sleep paralysis are not demonic entities, as was originally thought, but rather the person who has the experience. With this understanding comes an acknowledgment of the depth of our spiritual energy and how fully consuming it is. Perception, perception, perception. It is all a matter of how the experience is perceived. The extent to which this continual flow of energy impacts us 24/7, vibrating and connecting with every cell in our bodies, shaping our realities and influencing us from a different, energetic realm—a realm which has the capacity to be omnipresent and omnipotent for your benefit—is wondrous. Recognizing and appreciating your role in this energetic realm is crucial, and moving forward, this is what you are to be focused on. Imagine your power if you were to fully understand and be able to influence this energetic realm. Out of body experiences would be the tip of the iceberg as you came to realize that you can be, do, and have anything. You would know the future and the past as your untapped abilities were heightened and you connected with the higher vibrating energies. These are the gifts that we will speak of later, but for now, embrace the awakening and look forward to the changes and events which are taking place for your benefit.

As you begin to take back your power, your fear reduces and your confidence increases. The more you engage in the practices, the more your vibration increases and the more self-aware you become. You begin to leave behind negative, emotionally draining, and pessimistic thoughts and replace them with contemplation, introspection, and self-analysis. The focus in life becomes "you" as a priceless piece of art that you are sculpting into a magnificent masterpiece, as you begin to change internally to affect the external world. And that's very well done as we move into the next chapter to explore how to shift our focus from negative to positive and change a terrifying experience into an empowering reality.

## Affirmations to Practice:

- I now know that I was chosen to receive these valuable gifts and appreciate all that I am about to receive

- I am undeniably loved and can feel the care and support of the energies around me

# Chapter 5. Shifting Your Frequency

*A* major shift has taken place. You are now aware more than ever that you are spiritual energy in a physical body and that you are emitting a frequency that is attracting additional energy to you. Spiritual energy and its constitution are not something that is taught in everyday schools, so it is expected that the vast majority of us are unaware of its existence and therefore spend time researching this concept in order to understand it. What is important is that you have shown interest in this new language; you are attracted to content which will progress your spiritual understanding.

Now we will explore what it means to shift your frequency so that you can be attuned to the spiritual energy that is attempting to make contact with you during episodes of sleep paralysis. As I've already discussed, source energy vibrates at a very high frequency, and raising your own frequency is essential in order to receive the gifts that it's offering. It is the central piece around which everything else revolves. But how do you achieve this?

Raising your frequency is not physically difficult, but it does take consistency in applying the practices. Spiritual changes are taking place, and the physical manifestation of your efforts will be seen in time. That's how manifestation works: everything is manifested in the nonphysical realm before it is visible in our physical realm. The raising of your vibration takes place subtly without any immediate physical changes. For now, take heart in knowing that the practices are making changes to you that cannot be seen with the eyes.

Generally speaking, the work involves slight changes to your routine that are detailed in Part Three. They are designed to raise your frequency incrementally, recognizing that your frequency cannot permanently decrease. (Once it has increased it may momentarily decrease, with the potential to return to its original higher state). This chapter explores this process in greater detail, including how your perceptions influence your frequency and how changes to your frequency will impact your sleep as well as other aspects of your life.

# LIKE ATTRACTS LIKE: THE LAW OF ATTRACTION

To understand how to raise your frequency, it's important to understand the wonderful Law of Attraction. This is one of several laws that manage our connection and experience with the physical and nonphysical realms. It states simply that "that which is alike itself is attracted." For example, if you are feeling grumpy, situations will come into your orbit to match your feeling. The spiritual interpretation is that frequencies and their associated vibrations attract that which is of the same frequency. Whatever you are feeling will be physically manifested once you are paying attention and able to see it.

Your vibrational frequency acts like a magnet. Consciously or unconsciously, you send it out into the infinite Universe and it attracts that which is like itself. Moment by moment emotions such as happiness or sadness are sent out, as well as deep rooted emotions such as feelings of unworthiness, insecurities, or feelings of inadequacy. It is these lower energy vibrations that attract sleep paralysis. The lower vibrating frequencies are being emitted by you creating negative perceptions and experiences. Whatever the reason for your feelings, they can be changed. You have the choice to remain where you are or raise your vibration to a higher frequency and change the nature of what you are attracting. This involves moving yourself from your current comfort zone.

# PAYING ATTENTION

Something the Law of Attraction teaches us is that despite appearances, life—events, situations, and moments—doesn't just happen to us as if by magic. We are active participants, creating it all through our perception and vibrational frequency. We are the master creators, working in tandem with the spiritual energy that surrounds us and the wider Universal energy. We dictate everything, regardless of the effect that it has on us. It's actually quite good to know this and it places you firmly in the driver's seat.

The next time that you have an episode of sleep paralysis, pay attention to what led up to it. What have you been thinking about recently? What have you been involved in? Have you been relaxed or relatively stressed? How have people around you been responding? What has been your perception towards these things? What has been showing up in your life prior to the episode? By paying attention you begin to see a correlation with the things that have been taking place, your perception towards them, and your level of resistance. Each of these are contributing to your sleep paralysis episode, as you continue to disallow the positive energy from flowing freely within you, thereby creating disharmony.

As your life reflects back to you your feelings and emotions, your spiritual compass demonstrates your level of ease or restrictions in the moment. What you're doing here is shifting the spiritual compass to a more flexible position. This will not only remove your sleep paralysis, but also give you an enhanced sleeping experience. Paying attention to what is taking place around you is paramount; it can be used as your guide and lets you know when to take stock.

## PERCEPTION AND EMPOWERMENT

The level that your vibration or frequency can attain is endless, with the highest frequency being that of the Universal Source Creator. We are all striving at some point to be more, know more, feel more, and achieve more. It's called being human and it's part of our very makeup. The constant calling to be more is the Universal call for abundance in all things. Growth, learning, and expansion is what we are here for. There are no limits to what we can achieve, whether it has been physically manifested or remains in the nonphysical vibrational realm.

Taking care of yourself, then becomes paramount. The internal work becomes your physical reality as you begin to allow perceptions into your life that were previously blocked. Clearing these blockages therefore opens the door to an array of experiences, as you broaden your horizons and explore parts of yourself that were previously hidden. This is empowerment. You are taking back your power over your nights, your days—your very life. You are on the path to no longer feeling victimized by sleep paralysis and to being in control of yourself physically and spiritually.

This recognition of your self-empowerment in itself raises your vibration higher, as you seek clarity and knowledge. You have begun the process of transformation by allowing yourself to think and perceive differently and to consider alternative perspectives and concepts. Your feelings of self-worth and your self-perception will now be under scrutiny as this process examines who you are and who you think you are. Insecurities are exposed as your understanding of your personal battle with sleep paralysis takes shape.

Once the decision is made to take ownership and responsibility for all that takes place within and outside of you, your world opens and you begin to see things much clearer. It's no longer about the sleep paralysis, but your total existence in the Universe and your role within it. You begin to experience and understand yourself as a spiritual being before that of being physical and with this comes a fundamental paradigm shift.

## THE IMPACT OF RAISING YOUR FREQUENCY

It's a win-win situation. When you raise your frequency you feel happier, life holds excitement, you anticipate wellbeing, and as a consequence of the Law of Attraction, that is what you receive. You are in good health and "good spirits," as the saying goes, and you look forward to each day being filled with "positive vibes" and love. To feel this way is a joy for anyone. When you feel the essence of this joy the energies around you respond to your elevation, and there are changes in the nature of the sleep realm energies and your perception of them. Your heightened frequency aligns with that of the spiritual energy in a symbiotic relationship.

Gradually, you begin to notice that you feel a lot calmer and more relaxed. Situations that would normally bring discomfort are no longer important, and you begin to distance yourself from drama and conflict. Your overall sense of well being increases, as does your health.

While these changes are taking place, you begin to focus on you, naturally. You want to do things that you enjoy, your physical space is designed how you like it, the world begins to revolve around you, and you recognize that it is there to give you pleasure. Negative or non-aligned people, places, habits, and behaviors begin to disappear from your orbit as your vibration increases beyond them and then the magic begins.

As you begin to come into your power, it is acknowledged by the Universe, which responds accordingly. You take notice of things that take place around you and you begin to know your power. Reverberations take place as you vibrate at a higher frequency. These reverberations are now a core part of you as they interact with you through your physical and nonphysical being. This is the process that changes thoughts into things and it makes no difference whether it is day or night, whether you are awake or dreaming. The vibrations continue. It is now that you are able to more clearly interpret the events that take place during the sleep phase.

The process of increasing your frequency enhances your clarity, perception, and understanding of the wider world. Now when you sleep, your perception of the experience changes and so too does the experience itself. During your sleep, you become an active experiencer rather than a passive submissive; you are determined to unravel the events which are taking place while you sleep. It is your increased frequency which now allows you to interact with the nonphysical energies from a different perspective during the sleep state.

## CONCLUSION

If you have reached this point in the zine, substantial shifts in your perception have taken place, even if you are not aware of them. You have taken on new and perhaps different types of information that have influenced your view of sleep paralysis and how it has affected you. It's my intention that you begin to feel empowered and inquisitive in regards to your sleep paralysis experiences as we now move into practical steps that you can take to move confidently forward.

**Affirmations to Practice:**
- I seek to raise my vibration in joyous anticipation
- I willingly accept the gifts that are being offered

# PART THREE: ACTION STEPS

## *Introduction*

During your journey with sleep paralysis, there are practices and actions that you can incorporate into your daily life to embrace and transition past the sleep paralysis episode. These practices aid in the reduction of negative energy and support your spiritual development. The list that follows is not in a specific order and it is recommended that you read the list and plan when and how to include the actions in your daily schedule. Mornings are the best time to undertake practices, before the day gains momentum and distractions take place.

## ACTION STEP 1: SETTING INTENTIONS

You will only ever receive that which you have asked for, verbally or nonverbally, be it positive or negative. While your ability to receive sleep paralysis was determined prior to your birth by virtue of your spiritual development and lessons to be learnt during this lifetime, your request or calling for your spiritual development was made some time ago.

During this lifetime, you may have found yourself asking questions, reading books, or searching for information relating to anything from your general personal development to your spiritual development, and you may have found that your calling has been answered. To further your development and transcend sleep paralysis the intention must be constant, focused, and clear without any uncertainty or wobble. Without this you risk remaining with sleep paralysis, unable to transcend it.

### Follow this formula: Clarity, State, Expect, Relax

- Clarity. Know without any doubt that you want to transcend sleep paralysis. Be clear about why you want to transcend it and establish a positive expectation.

- State. Write down your intention, including why you want it, and verbally repeat it daily.

- Expect. Prepare to transcend sleep paralysis, anticipate it and look forward to it.

- Relax. Do not set a deadline or date by which this should take place. Let the Universe and your nonphysical counterparts take over. Your role is to know that it will take place.

## ACTION STEP 2: STOP THE NEGATIVE SELF-TALK

Most of us speak negatively about ourselves at some time. We vocalize it and say things to ourselves. For example, "There's no point even trying, I'm not going to get it anyway," or "They'll never consider me." We even make statements that suggest that we are not intelligent, attractive, or sophisticated enough.

We have formed and perpetuated these habits over time. With these thoughts, it is harder to love ourselves or break the cycle of low self-esteem and confidence. It's now more important than ever not to think negative thoughts. You can learn to stop the negative self-talk and love yourself by being supportive and encouraging to yourself. This helps release the pressure that we have placed on ourselves. Accept yourself where you are, the way you are. Remember that you are special and perfectly loved.

### Follow this formula: Notice, Interrupt, Replace, Repeat

- Notice. The first step in removing the negative self-talk is to notice when you are doing it. Whether you are saying it to someone or thinking it, pay attention to when it happens. You are likely on autopilot throughout the day as you constantly chatter, make excuses, and negatively self-talk.

- Interrupt. The moment you notice it, immediately stop speaking or thinking the words. Change the subject and the thought will dissipate instantly. You'll be surprised at how quickly a thought can change.

- Replace. You can then replace the thought with a softer, supportive, less critical, and more positive thought. So rather than saying, "I've never been able to do this and don't think I ever will," say, "I will do the best that I can. I am allowed to make mistakes and each day I will do a little better than yesterday. Wherever I am is all right."

- Repeat. Practice this daily, and it will become easier each time to catch the thought early, before it has had an opportunity to gather momentum.

## ACTION STEP 3: SPEND TIME DOING SOMETHING YOU LOVE

When was the last time you spent time alone doing something just for you? Something that you enjoy doing, something that you never seem to get around to doing? It may even have been so long ago that you have forgotten what you love to do. Many of us have become so busy that we find very little time for ourselves. In between home, work, family, and parenting, there is not much time left over.

Spending time alone is extremely healthy and teaches us to enjoy solitude. It allows us to spend time internally, enjoying emotions and feelings inspired by ourselves, which strengthens our self-worth. Spending time doing something we love brings additional value. Whether it be eating at a particular restaurant or preparing yourself a certain type of food, watching a movie or listening to music, or doing something creative, make a conscious effort each week to make time on your calendar for you. Plan the time in the same way that you would plan a special date. Prepare for it, bask in the anticipation of it, and do it undisturbed, without any distractions.

This enhances the practice of mindfulness. We allow ourselves to do things that focus us in the moment. We are not thinking about what has happened in the past or what is going to take place tomorrow. Instead, we enjoy the feeling of anticipation and the preparation. Being in the moment reduces anxiety and stress. Remember that you love yourself, so this is an opportunity to show it.

## Follow this formula: Select, Allocate, Prepare, Immerse

- Select. Choose somewhere or something that excites you. Something that you would love to do so that you anticipate and look forward to it.

- Allocate. Set aside at least two hours to enjoy your activity. Remove all distractions such as telephones, televisions, laptops, and other people. You must be alone and in an environment that is quiet.

- Prepare. Before beginning your activity, stand or sit motionless for ten minutes and look around your environment. What do you see? Has anything in particular caught your attention? Describe it to yourself. Look in detail at it again and describe it, this time seeing beyond the obvious. How does it make you feel? Savor the feelings.

- Immerse. When you are ready, enjoy your chosen activity. Spend the entire time allocated; do not cut yourself short. Allow yourself to be completely immersed in the moment.

## ACTION STEP 4: CREATE A HEALTHY ENVIRONMENT
Just like flowers need a healthy, well maintained environment to bloom, so do you. Your environment must be carefully selected to produce the best

you. An environment where you feel scrutinized, pressured, critiqued, or judged is not healthy and cannot allow the inner you to bloom. This can be difficult, as you may have lived in a subtly or not-so-subtly unhealthy environment for most of your life.

So, it's important to look at your environment and see who may be making it unhealthy. It may be family, friends, or colleagues. Regardless of who it is, you need to avoid them and remove yourself from this environment. It does not serve you well and provides no benefit to the inner you. Spend time with people who facilitate your inner development and give you the recognition and space to develop. In this environment you will feel renewed, alive, and able to express the inner you, sharing with peers and contributing to the development of each other's inner self.

You are taking care of you now, and that must be a priority. Do not give into guilt or remorse. Others may even try to pressure you into staying in their circle. It is also critical to allow people to say what they want to say about you. It is their prerogative. It is none of your business what they want to say about you. Your value comes from within, not from the external. You are now on a different path and cannot allow yourself to be among people who don't support your expansion.

**Follow this formula: Observe, Remove Yourself, Shift Away**
- Observe. Begin to pay attention to how you feel in situations where you are spending time with others.

- Remove Yourself. If you feel any discomfort, tactfully remove yourself from the situation or politely turn down an invitation.

- Shift Away. Gradually, over time, you will filter out the people who are not matched to you emotionally and spiritually as you refuse to share your time and space with anyone who does not make you feel comfortable.

## ACTION STEP 5: YOU DON'T HAVE TO FIGHT ALONE
There will always be nay-sayers who doubt what you are doing and will not hesitate to let you know. There are times when you stop speaking up and are less likely to take a chance as your inner critic replays the words which someone has said.

On a positive note, if someone is analyzing you to the extent that they have negative comments about you, there must be something about you which has drawn their attention. Something they have seen highlights their own self-doubts, which are then projected onto you. Their concerns really have nothing to do with you, but say a lot about them.

When the perception of others affects your inner self, it is important to stay focused and believe in yourself. You do not need external validation and most importantly you do not need to go through this transformation alone. In this modern world of technology, there are many groups that can be joined to support your growth. These groups are of like-minded peers and confidants who have been exactly where you are.

Join at least one spiritually-minded group and consistently contribute to the group, seeking support when you need it. Ensure that you check the validity of the group before you join it and once you're sure that it meets your needs, regularly check in, get up to date, and participate. This will support not only you, but other group members. This group may be local and in-person, but luckily, in today's world of social media and the internet, it may also be online. Specialized online groups can help connect you with people who may not be available in your local area.

### Follow this formula: Envision, Search, Join, Participate

- Envision. Consider what type of support you would like. It may be to join a meditation group to help with daily meditation, a spiritual awareness group to help with questions and advice, or a sleep paralysis group where you can share your experience.

- Search. Use a medium such as Facebook or LinkedIn, or search the Internet for forums that you can join. Remember that you are looking for a credible, reputable website. Before joining, research the group to ensure that it meets your needs, and has appropriate privacy systems in place.

- Join. Join the group and spend up to a few weeks observing the way it is used by others. Make sure it feels safe and supportive, and make sure it matches what you envisioned.

- Participate. Begin to take part in the group, by posting comments, concerns, questions, as well as providing support for others.

## ACTION STEP 6: MEDITATE, MEDITATE, MEDITATE

Meditation is a technique used to connect with your inner self more deeply, and it can help bring a sense of peace. It will give you lower levels of stress, increased awareness, and stronger intuition. Any way you choose to meditate is fine. I prefer to use a guided meditation in the form of a sound recording on my phone. Whatever helps you relax the most will help you achieve optimal results. There is no right or wrong way to meditate.

## Follow this formula: Prepare, Find Your Seat, Begin

- Prepare. Pick a spot in your home that is relaxing to you. You can sit on the ground, a cushion, a chair, a sofa, or even your bed. You can also sit in nature if you like.

- Find Your Seat. Try to sit with your spine straight and your hands relaxed in your lap. If you are in a chair, sit with your feet planted firmly on the ground, knees and ankles uncrossed. If you are seated elsewhere, you may sit with crossed legs or however is most comfortable.

- Begin. Close your eyes. Imagine a sense of calm. Try to breathe it in. Inhale calm, exhale worry. Continue for five minutes. If the mind is still racing, you can try putting on some relaxing music to help enhance your technique. As you become better at this, increase your time gradually.

# ACTION STEP 7: CULTIVATE AN ATTITUDE OF APPRECIATION

We know that it's important to express gratitude and appreciation. In addition to being socially appropriate, an attitude of appreciation also has spiritual attributes that often go overlooked.

When you're in a state of appreciation you raise your vibration, and in the raising of your vibration you align with energies that allow your health and happiness to flourish. In those moments you align with source love and positivity, and the most wonderful part of all is that the more you express and feel appreciation, the more things you have in your life to appreciate, thereby creating an energy of joy, peace, satisfaction, and contentment within and around you.

## Follow this formula: Appreciate, Appreciate, Appreciate

- Appreciate. First thing in the morning, make a list of five things that you appreciate.

- Appreciate. Beside each one, write down why you appreciate it. As you write, visualize it and allow yourself to feel the appreciation. Do not resist the emotion, let it flow within you.

- Appreciate. As your day progresses, pay attention to things that you appreciate and allow these emotions to move within you for a minimum of 40 seconds.

## ACTION STEP 8: HIGHER SELF-CONNECTION

What if you could connect with your higher self to hear the wisdom that it offers you directly? Your higher self, the energy part of you that connects with all that is, is always there with you wanting only the best for you.

The unity with your higher self strengthens your physical and nonphysical connection with infinity, thereby giving you greater control that facilitates your transcending sleep paralysis. Do this practice every morning before your day begins.

### Follow this formula: Relax, Timer, Within, Listen

- Relax. Prepare yourself as you would if you were meditating. Ensure that external noise is as minimal as possible.

- Timer. Set your timer for fifteen minutes, close your eyes and relax.

- Within. With your eyes closed, pay attention to what you see; lights, movements, shapes, and colors.

- Listen. Listen to the internal sounds that your body makes. Can you hear your heartbeat, muscle movements, or stomach? Allow thoughts to come into your mind. They will appear on their own. Continue to listen internally, paying attention to the internal communication.

## ACTION STEP 9: THE POWER OF NATURE'S ENERGY

We all love being in nature. It has a serene ability to calm and relax you regardless of the environment that you choose.

Environments where things grow are filled with abundance. Energy flows freely as the environment thrives without restriction. This abundant energy does not have limiting beliefs, fears, or anxieties. It is in its natural state of love, which is abundant. This abundance is so rampant that we attempt to control and reduce it.

The day to day environments that we live in can be restrictive and contain energies which do not serve us. To be amidst pure natural energies can have a refreshing affect upon you, which enables the renewing of your core energy.

**Follow this formula: Choose, Stay, Relax**

- Choose. Choose your ideal environment, one that you can access regularly.

- Stay. Stay for at least one hour in this environment alone each day.

- Relax. While you are there, do light tasks such as reading something that you enjoy, or paying attention to the scenery. It's important not to engage in activities that cause stress or negative emotions while you're in this environment. Allow the experience to be as pleasurable and scenic as possible.

## ACTION STEP 10: SLEEP PARALYSIS JOURNAL

Journaling has so many benefits and can be used in so many different ways.

Apart from helping you with the many daily stresses, it can help you move forward positively and bring your plans into reality. By getting all of your emotions onto paper, you express yourself and bring clarity and focus to any given situation. You release tensions and resistance to particular issues while highlighting irregularities, feelings, and hidden patterns of behavior. It's also a diary, a personal written record by date that captures a situation as it unfolds. You can savor it and look at your progress with satisfaction, recognizing your changes and feelings over time.

While journaling is a great tool generally, for this specific journaling practice you'll be recording your feelings towards sleep paralysis. If you have any episodes of sleep paralysis, record them here, and this includes all the things that took place during your sleep paralysis episode. Record your plans to transcend sleep paralysis and what you are doing to carry them out. Record the changes that you notice in yourself as well as the spiritual gifts that are unfolding.

**Follow this formula: Journal, Write, Free Flow**

- Journal. Choose a specific notebook to record your journal entries in. This need not be an expensive book, but it must give you the feeling of it being a special book to write in. Today journals do not have to be physical books, they can be online, but remember to make it special.

- Write. Find a private space, at a time that feels right for you. This can be everyday, or every two to three days. You can either make it a part of your daily routine or write when the need arises. Don't worry about your handwriting, spelling, or grammar. You're the only one reading the journal. Protect your privacy and keep your journal in a safe and private place.

- Free Flow. Write about your feelings and end the entry on a positive note. Date each journal entry; this is important for when you are looking back. Write in free flow, keep it simple and natural, and don't stop. Just let the words flow.

## ACTION STEP 11: THE ART OF SELF-LOVE

Loving yourself is at the heart of your spiritual connection. Love is the primary emotion of Source or the Creator, and love of self is high on the list of things to achieve to transcend sleep paralysis. Love is the emotion that timelessly creates abundance, growth, and progress. Look at your garden: whether or not you maintain it, growth will still take place. This is due to the boundless love of the Creator, which is eternal.

At times, we extend love to others and things around us but forget to show ourselves that love. As individuals we require it to live in a balanced and harmonious way, for without loving yourself how can you truly love others? That's also the quandary for those that experience sleep paralysis. Much is given to others to the detriment of self, and the sleep paralysis episodes are a wakeup call to prioritize your needs and show yourself love.

### Follow this formula: First, Say no, Forgive
- First. Before you get out of bed, tell yourself three positive things. Feel them, believe them, and know them. Fill yourself with self-confidence.
- Say No. Learn to say no. Say it often without guilt or apology.
- Forgive yourself for things that you or others think you have done. The past remains unchanged, and it is now time to move on and unchain yourself.

## ACTION STEP 12: ANOTHER APPROACH TO SELF-LOVE

Loving yourself is essential, not just for the sleep paralysis experiencer, but in general. Self-worth, self-compassion, and self-empowerment all stem from self-love and yes, it's essential to cultivate if you plan to overcome sleep paralysis. If you were asked to name five things that you love about yourself what would they be? This is the essence of this practice, the epitome of self-love. We all have qualities that we admire about ourselves. It doesn't matter what anyone else thinks, it's what you think that truly matters.

### Follow this formula: Love, Self, Love

- On a sheet of paper draw two columns.
- Love. Write down five things that you love about yourself in one column.
- Self. In the other column, explain why you love each of these things about yourself.
- Love. Repeat this exercise every two days, finding new things to love about you each time.

## ACTION STEP 13: SHIFTING MINDSET

A lot goes on in the mind that is directly linked to sleep paralysis. Much of your experience can be traced back to your thoughts, beliefs, and overall mindset, which have been formed over a lifetime. We are on a journey to change your mindset, which has become focussed negatively on sleep paralysis. Your mindset keeps you in the same place like a ship docked at port. Thoughts are repeated, assumptions are believed, and you believe the reality that is before you without considering that an alternative exists. We are now reeling in the anchor and allowing the ship to set sail and drift off into the horizon.

You are the master of your mindset, and you have the tools with which to change it. Much of what we are doing now is part of the mindset change, which has a nonphysical effect on the nonphysical you and the vibration that you emit.

### Follow this formula: Change, Learn, Set

- Change your self-talk about sleep paralysis. Instead of framing it as something negative, frame it as something positive, with endless possibilities waiting to be explored.
- Learn about your spirituality. Read books, listen to podcasts, and watch shows that support your positive personal spiritual development.
- Set your mindset. Evaluate yourself to determine what you need, then work towards it.

## ACTION STEP 14: GET ANGRY

Anger is normally seen as a negative emotion, yet in this situation it can be positive and wholesome, strengthening your internal emotional muscle and demonstrating and affirming your self-love. When you are angry and direct your anger towards whatever you experience during sleep paralysis, you are standing up for yourself. This conveys the message that you care enough for yourself to take an assertive stand for the rights of you.

You have permission to be angry, as long as you don't hurt or negatively impact anyone. This anger is then taken energetically into your sleep state and is communicated to the nonphysical energies that you engage with while you sleep.

### Follow this formula: Write, Sing, Dance, Draw

- Write out your anger. Using your journal is a wonderful way to do this, allowing the anger to flow through the pen onto the paper.

- Sing, dance, or draw the anger, releasing it as expressively as possible.

- In all cases, feel the anger as you express it. Don't try to limit or subdue it.

## ACTION STEP 15: DREAM DIARY

Dreams take place each time that you sleep regardless of the sleep paralysis episode. Your nonphysical body engages in numerous activities, events, and conversations in many different realms. Here, time and space are nonexistent and your nonphysical body has the omnipresent ability to be in several places simultaneously.

The energetic gap between the sleep and waking states keeps what takes place while you sleep separated from what happens when you are awake. The fear that is experienced during the sleep paralysis episode and the speed of the waking up process leaves a sufficient impression to ensure that the sleep paralysis is remembered when you awake, as you recall the negative emotions first. Your nonphysical self quickly rejoins your physical body at the same time as your awakening.

The normal dream state does not provide the intensity of the emotions felt during sleep paralysis, which is why most of your dreams are not recalled. The separation between the awake and sleep state is too energetically different.

In fact, your strengthened connection with your higher self can make the remembering of your dreams easier, or put another way, you are able to recall your experiences of the nonphysical realm more easily when you are more connected to your higher self. And of course, you must set the intention to do so.

This ability to recall your dreams will be needed in your transcendence of sleep paralysis. As the sleep paralysis episodes reduce, you will also be uncovering your ability to non-physically connect with other realms while you sleep, and these experiences will be recorded in your dream diary. This is not a record of your sleep paralysis. Your Sleep Paralysis Journal captures those experiences. This is specifically for the dream experience.

### Follow this formula: Journal, Write, Record, Review

- Journal. Keeping a specific dream journal becomes an important tool in understanding your nonphysical activity while you sleep.

- Write. Keep it by your bed together with a pen or pencil so that as soon as you awake you can record your experience.

- Record. When you awaken, it is important to record not only the events that took place in your sleep state, but your emotions as well. Your emotions during the dream gives you clues about the overall experience.

- Review. Monitor your dream experience by reviewing your dream journal over time, and pay attention to what you are experiencing.

## ACTION STEP 16: AWAKEN SLOWLY

Waking up and not immediately getting out of bed can be an art. Many of us have responsibilities that mean waking up and getting into action. Whether it's children, work, or other commitments, we arise with a "jump," immediately picking up from where we left off the previous day. For those that experience sleep paralysis, this action validates that we are on autopilot and committed to following our internal programming.

The process of waking up slowly allows time to change the program and know that this is truly a new day that you have the ability to influence and control. This too is taking back your power, broadening your mindset, and strengthening your spiritual muscle, placing you firmly in the driver's seat.

### Follow this formula: Refresh, Stay, Feel, Listen

- Refresh. If possible, awaken half an hour earlier than you need to. Try to ensure that no one else in your household is awake. It is important to awaken slowly, recalling as much of the sleep state experience as possible and prolonging the sensation to create a bridge between the sleep and waking states.

- Stay. When you awaken, remain in bed.

- Feel. Allow yourself to feel the sensation of the bed, its sheets and how this feels against your skin. Savor the feeling as you relax and enjoy the pleasantness. Give no thought to the things that need to be done in the forthcoming day.

- Listen to the sounds around you and where they are coming from. Savour and relish the relaxing experience. Focus on positive things mentally, as this helps to increase your vibration, and notice the pleasurable things around you, expressing appreciation mentally.

## ACTION STEP 17: DELIBERATELY EMBELLISH YOUR THINKING

You can deliberately raise your vibration at regular intervals by monitoring your thoughts and specifically choosing to create a reality that brings you joy and pleasure.

When we have positive experiences our vibration peaks for a period of time. This peak is not sustained, unless the emotion is sustained for at least thirty seconds, thereby allowing its energy time to interface with similarly aligned energy, creating a cascading effect. Regularly recalling positive experiences and emotions enables a sustained vibration supported by "like energies." Your vibration can then continue to increase, changing the frequency you emit and your perception and experience of sleep paralysis. This frequency stays with you during your sleep state.

### Follow this formula: Recall, Savor

- Recall an event that gives you satisfaction. In the recall, focus on your feelings and emotions. While recalling the experience, ask yourself the following questions: What specifically gave you pleasure? How did it make you feel? Why did it make you feel this way?

- Savor and relish the feelings. Let the recall last a minimum of thirty seconds.

# ACTION STEP 18: SENSING SURROUNDING ENERGIES

You are a multi-perceptive being who can experience far more than what you have been led to believe. As human beings, our perception focuses on the things which our five senses demonstrate to us, combined with information related to our belief system, logic, and mindset, to arrive at a specific conclusion.

Anyone who experiences sleep paralysis has the ability to use more than the five senses to experience and perceive Universal dimensions and translate what is perceived meaningfully. When you awaken and strengthen your spiritual core, these abilities will surface and provide you with an additional understanding of the role of sleep paralysis and your role within the wider Universe.

## Follow this formula: Connect, Awareness, Note

- Connect. The combined efforts of meditation, raising your vibration, and shifting your mindset allow you to connect with nonphysical energy in a way that you can perceive, translate, and accept. The awareness of nonphysical energy is subtle and you cannot fully explore it.

- Awareness. Pay attention to your feelings and the things you hear and see, no matter how extreme they may seem. Set the intention that you want to perceive and understand nonphysical energy.

- Note. You may see colors or sparks of light, hear sounds that seem to have come from nowhere, or smell wafts of different scents. Note that these relate to spiritual gifts such as clairaudience (clear hearing), clairscent (clear smelling) and clairvoyance (clear vision or seeing).

# Conclusion: Moving Forward to Victory

*T*ogether we have covered a lot of ground and many changes have taken place, within and external to you. You have come far in terms of your understanding of sleep paralysis and your own spirituality. Feel proud that you have made it this far and that you have sustained the intention to learn and understand more. You are being uniquely positioned to transcend sleep paralysis and have more control of your day-to-day life.

The foreboding sleep state entities are no longer frightening as your nonphysical spiritual muscle is strengthening its level of understanding and breadth of perception. The glass is no longer half empty, but half full as you can now witness the experience for what it is: a spiritual engagement, your spiritual engagement.

You are no longer the sufferer of the experience, suffering alone in silence, terrified to sleep, devoid of healthy rest, but an active participant in this journey that is taking you to a new place. A place of exploration and insight. A place that has lain dormant on your periphery while actively anticipating your arrival. These are exciting times. You are on the edges of a new world, a new dawn, quite literally a new awakening. And you get to experience it all.

You have shown courage, faith, the ability to follow your intuition, which was telling you that something was wrong, and most of all the willingness to step aside from the crowd and embrace your true potential. This should be celebrated. Perhaps a private celebration should be had as you now go beyond the masses into that unique place where persons with enhanced and sustained enlightenment go. A place beyond all that we currently know. You are expanding thought, expanding realities, and bringing in a dawn. I feel especially proud to be a part of this new age, as well as being able to share what I know to help people along the way. I can see beyond the horizon as we move into the light. Things would be a lot simpler if I could say to you that the end is in sight, but I can't as there is no end. There is only more and more enlightenment and understanding. When it comes to spirituality, we each start from where we are, and that's okay. There are no judgments and no expectations. The goal is acceptance of where you are and what you know. From here on in you will be continually expanding and going beyond your personal boundaries of spiritual understanding and experience. Here, the rules are being learned while you're engaged in the action, and they are not the same for everyone. The only guarantee is that as you move forward you will surpass yourself. Your health and wellbeing will improve dramatically, and you will be more fulfilled and content with life. By coming to understand the power of your sleep paralysis, you will blossom as your spirit shines and announces the person you really are.